HOW TO BEAR
YOUR TEETH
AT STRANGERS

©2021 Amon Elise

World Stage Press

How To Bear Your Teeth At Strangers

ISBN-13: 978-1-952952-12-8

First Edition, 2021

Author Photo by Gennifer Caesar

HOW TO BEAR
YOUR TEETH
AT STRANGERS

World Stage Press
Verse from the Village

Amon Elise

For the women who have forgotten how to carry their teeth, without which, their voices would not be heard the same. And, of course, for my momma.

Table of Contents

Primary

(an opening)

A new tooth emerging from the gums is called an eruption. I like the idea of something sharp, almost weaponized, arising from soft, raw flesh. We get twenty chances to attack life head on, to tear off whole chunks of the world and chew it over. Then when you've bit down too hard and the grind is too much to bear, your first set of teeth begin to fall out leaving gaping lessons for you to obsess and tongue over. By design.

Incisors

A smile is an act of submission, my lips unveiling a shield of non-confrontational intentions. The flash is so brief that all you might remember are my incisors. They are meant to cut and hold objects for digestion. Mainly food, but also sometimes words. Words I didn't say when I had the chance. Words I didn't say because they wouldn't be heard. Words I didn't say because I was too afraid of living outside the first impression. Afraid of not being loved after I opened my mouth.

The Existential We

When We includes you,
I forget about the passing of another.
I can relish that a victory anywhere
is a victory everywhere,
and more importantly, mine.
I can cry for a pain
we felt seven skins away
but never far removed.
That my inhale is just
someone else's exhale
recycled.
That which was them,
in me now,
a We.
It must look like a chaos of mirrors reflecting the reflections
of reflections of themselves.
At their center, a darkness
of all colors,
a mixed context
without owner
amongst all.
Shared.
With the passing of our time
all I can hope is my darkness goes
unrecognized
as belonging to me.
I must assume
you saw it too,
in your innards
even while so far removed.
A speculum of effigy,
I bequeath you
a We.

Filtered

I want to bury myself into your side.
I want to make myself really small and insignificant.
I want to fit under your arm,
let you dry me out
between the thinnest of papers.
Funny how they can hold so much context.
Preach me
in a different language.
My audience has never quite understood me
anyway.
I just want more.
I wonder if Eve ever felt this way,
if she lived
in the shadow of Lilith,
a full female standing in her own form,
and realized the danger
of allowing men to tell her story.
Can't even fight her way
out of a different book,
that Lilith.
Wonder if they burnt her at the stake.
Not like we could find the ashes,
not even on a Wednesday.
I want more.
I wonder if Eve
isn't an adversary, but a conjoinment?
If they pointed a finger and discovered,
(I'm sorry) separated,
Lilith from our wombs.
And that's why we cleanse for seven days!
As long as it takes to build a universe.
We long to be bigger than any story you could ever
force in a book.
I want more.
I wonder if Eve
sat there looking at Lilith's banishment
and realized she had to find her own way
to get there.
And not even to save Lilith.

The Liliths of the world don't need saving.
It's the Eves of the world:
Willing to take a walk by herself.
Willing to trust a snake to escape an Adam.
Willing to eat knowledge to chase a Lilith.
Needing to smell a flower beyond her own garden.
I wonder if Eve ever stood on her own
(a solo chapter is a book after all)
and saw more comparisons than contrasts?
I wouldn't know,
for I am not Lilith,
or so the men have said.

Boundaries

There was a time
when I would consult you
before I took a breath.
A quick check
for approval
before I lost another piece of me.
Maybe the last.
You thought I hesitated.
In reality,
I flinched.

House Rules

Home was being small enough to sleep
on my chosen father's belly,
hear the whole world expand and collapse with his breath.
Mine would crush on his say so.
She left him.
He never left me.
Home was triple XL shirts and gym shorts
because the penises were visiting.
Home was He,
fixing the lightbulbs.
Home was Him,
ripping up carpet and
laying down wood
floors.
Home was His,
adding to the 13 television sets
to give us something else to watch.
Home was never allowing dogs in the house,
but there were always dogs in the home.
Never once a flea, though.
Performing tricks
like sit,
speak,
but don't stay.
They always went home to their own
cages.
Home was "don't make eye contact."
Home was distance.
Home was "watch the jokes you make
with the men,
and cross your legs."
Home was loud music past bedtime.
Home was rushed footsteps and
engines purring,
signaling another morning started.

Home had space for men
and no room for me,
so I left.

Tillandsia

My Venus
told me once
that she'll never be a flower.
And I, as her daughter,
am expected of more.
Denied the choice of division,
I am wrapped within her.
She spreads her vines
to confine who she chooses to keep.
Those flies don't even know they're devoured.
Forced to feed the undefeated,
I am supposed to grow in her shadow
and bloom before her.
As she grows older,
is it I who will loan her my nutrients
with these wisps of roots?
Evolved in air,
if I just wait for that final winter,
maybe my daughters
will have a chance
to learn the danger of soil.

*Tillandsia are commonly known as air plants

Black Privilege

My closed fist,
manicured nails clenched against palm
bursting against the very air.
My closed fist is sometimes
my ass spreading
on the torn cloth of a bus seat.
Mimicking his smile,
ripped apart,
spreading between us
from years of practice.
Everyone standing between us,
a set of stacked colors,
anything but a rainbow.
My closed fist is to sit next to his
6ft, 300 lbs,
who has been forced to bear two spaces
at the cost of one.
Not an inch of which has to do with his waistline.
I will give him the gift
of pretending he saved this seat for me.
Showing the lighter colors the darkness in their hearts.
Futile to change their minds,
but hoping the guilt
will stop a next time.
But this time,
not quite touching,
we will sit
together.

The Midnight Hour

Does anyone ever teach you how to love the Black boy?
Sometimes the Black men don't know how to come home.
Other times they are taken from you
in the midnight hour.
Hard to know if the freedom he's craving
is what's keeping him out tonight,
the freedom of empty streets
where he can be as large as he wants,
where his blackness can spread out thick,
exclaimed in smile,
or if the reason he can't come home
is because he's too busy escaping me.
Maybe I don't look like freedom to him
tonight.
Perhaps the last time I saw him
will be the last time I see him
for many many nights to come,
or did he fight tooth and nail to come back home to me?
And instead got swallowed up in light
like all the generations chasing freedom
before him.
Whole.

Confirmation

I saw I wasn't crazy,
in the way you mirrored
my two steps closer.
I breathed your air
for 26 seconds.
We reflected.
I wondered if your taste would be
as sweet
as the pineapple rum,
or if the moment had already been swallowed.
Turns out
our retreat
tastes like shattered opportunity.

Canines

It's important knowing to whom you can and can't show your teeth. Especially not the sharp ones. I don't remember the first time I talked back. I just know it sure as hell wasn't at my mother. These are the sharp poems. Poems I'll have to apologize for. The sharp corners of my mouth.

Daddyland Call Center Transcript 082264

[Redacted for Trainee use]

You've reached the Daddyland Hotline,
where there are absolutely no consequences to previously not using birth control.
Please hold.

[For the ones that need courage]
Thank you for holding.
Yes, contrary to popular belief, being fatherless has reached a state of normativity. They'll be fine! That's why they call them off-spring, get it? How old is the child? Oh - the children. That's fine. In fact, we've found the earlier the better, we'd even say easier. All you have to do is get in your car, abandon parenting, and drive.
Yes, just continue to do that until you reach us.
You'll know when you're here.
Everyone will.

[For the intake]
Why hello there, and welcome to Daddyland! We've been expecting you. Please place all cell phones, pagers, mailboxes, and firewood in those bins. Yes, we're serious. We can't risk having smoke signals reach you here. You did agree to the terms and conditions as they were read to you, yes? Now, how about you place all those pens, pencils, and paper in the incinerators to your left? Now you're all set. Fill up your time with the other would-be fathers! They like to... well no one knows what they like to do. It's a secret. But now you'll get the full experience.

[The first follow up. Have the price list ready. Costs are high and rising.]
Well, it's been a few months, and we're calling to check up on you. How has everything been? That's great to hear! May I interest you in some upgrades? We already have you down for the "talk through my lawyer" package, but I could suggest the "angry new wife" or "the randomized women" options. They are priced about the same. For the truly brave, I can offer you the "direct to disconnect" plan. And you're in luck! It looks like we have a huge sale on the "total deniability" package.
Oh well that's where we offer to sever your wrists.
That way the whole thing is really out of your hands.

[When they need to hear validation.]
Congratulations! It's been about [insert time frame here]. You didn't even notice the birthdays did you? Yeah, sometimes the abandoned family does stop trying to contact you at about this point, yes.

[At year one and every major interval. Don't worry, they won't notice the pattern.]
We hear you've hit a [insert milestone here], Old Timer! Oh, I'm sorry to hear about that. Unfortunately, we do not offer "Alternative Father Figure Blocking" packages. They were discontinued after several placebo trials. It didn't test well.
I'm sorry, we don't have Hallmark here.
We don't even recognize the third Sunday in June, sir.

[For when they step out.]
Hello? I hope we haven't contacted you at a bad time. But we're seeing some suspicious activity, and we just wanted to confirm: You tried to "reach out" to your biologicals two days prior? Let's talk about that. Why do you feel the need to comment on their lives now? We don't suggest contacting her, sorry. Especially not to deliver overdue praise. While we continue to promote diversity, we do not advise warning him about dating those women.

[For the repeat offenders.]
It's great to hear your voice. That call-interceptor program of ours does a great job doesn't it? Well now that we have you, we've seen some further concerns we really need to address. This is simply not good. Please consider all the positive influence you've had by not being there. You may disrupt their lives by trying to contact them now. No, our plans don't just expire because they're legal adults.
[allow time for their expletives here]
It was in the terms and conditions.

[For the persistent.]
Have you been receiving our messages? Do you still think it was a wise decision? I see you thought this through. We never took you to be a progressive. Yeah, well no one ever hears about them. We heard this is your third attempt at a restart. Yes, we're aware of the difficulties. Well we're always here if you need us, just a phone call away.

[For the successful.]
Hey, this is Daddyland calling to check in on you. Well you're one of the few

who managed to effectively opt out of our program. We'd like to ask how you're fairing for our weekly newsletter. A sort of "Where Are They Now" edition.

Graduated without debt? Peace Corps? Oh, but still writing poems about her emotions instead of being direct? And he's still ignoring your entire existence? Unforgiving, huh? Well that's unfortunate. Maybe it's just a phase. Like your absence from their life. I think that's rather rash, isn't it? Alright, I'll remove you immediately. Please let us know if we can be of further assistance.

Oh, unfortunately we don't have a listed contact for Fatherhood.

I'm sure it's something you and your children can figure out together.

Mister Mister

I want to tell my teacher
that he doesn't really know me,
that the look in his eyes
of exasperation
doesn't sorta show me
that the work on the board is even for me.
And every time
he attempts to discuss the N-word,
or how "they" feel,
and makes eye contact,
I have to subtract my fist
from an equation
that will lead to my personal devastation.
Because despite him – I'm gonna make it.
Proving my success so he'll have to take it.
Trust my grades show I don't fake it.
And if he's stupid enough
to throw a peace sign my way
at the end of the day,
I guess I'll be forced to sit and pray
behind a laugh hiding my insatiable anger,
hiding how truly close he is to danger.
And if on our final
he makes issues
about problems in the Black community
that he's only going to misuse,
sorta like he did on our mid-term,
I'm gonna have to hold back and hold firm
so I won't have to revert to my skills of taxiderm
and remain silent.
Exercising a choice
that he can't take from me,
despite how he degrades me,
with the silence of my voice.
Because a man had a dream one day,
and it's so sad that he was sleepin'.
If he came back I'm sure he'd be in the deep end,
to find all the problems he could wade knee deep in.
Choking on broken promises of presidents caught creepin'

around racial issues and words they should be keepin'.
So let me pause and back up,
back track, retrack, and crack up
over the assumption that my teacher is a racist.
His eyes are just filled with the prejudice.
Found in a world of black and white,
and the problem is that he isn't the only resident.
Lemme repeat – he isn't the only resident.
So welcome to the world of the gray,
filled with the social dissidents.
If you don't know
then here's your chance to get a hint:
Yeah – I'm a student of the IB.
In addition to the skin,
the message should equate to don't try me.
I got goals in different area codes,
back pains from the heaviest of work loads,
and with all my high aspirations
you choose to give me the look of constipation?
But I rephrase.
My teacher is not a racist.
He holds nothing against my color.
He's just following the knowledge he was told,
unknowingly putting on the blindfold.
I know it's hard,
but please disregard
all others previous behavior
when you refer to me.
I am not a copy.
Let me introduce you to the blueprint
of a structure so tall,
in the sun you'd have to squint
to see me – but you're already blind.
But I need you to see me.
Push, tease, and guarantee me
a future.
As a teacher,
only through your hands
is success a main feature
of my life.
And if you treat me as a rerun,
all of your actions redone,

losing myself as the web is respun,
then I've already lost a battle
that he's already won.
So I'm cast out of an opportunity.
Washing down the drain fluidly.
Lost because prejudiced eyes don't find my skin keen,
and thus darkens the future that was never once seen.

Non-starters for My Non-starter

Hi.

He's 19,
but I'll do his resume for him anyway.
Try not to remember a pack of Skittles and some Sprite.
My favorites
are enough to keep him from justice.
To keep him from coming home bearing gifts
for once.

Your cheeks are sinking.
Where did we go wrong?
You don't have a single father figure in jail.

Stop chasing those white girls.

I could write this,
but mama won't let it leave the house.

Masculinity isn't something you can spoonfeed.

If our dad was around,
maybe it would be enough to talk about
who failed to raise you.
That guilt certainly cannot be mine.

Suffering White boy problems with Black boy results.

Where do I fit the pause of breath
Mom had
when they asked that girl
if you raped her?
Feeling like a fresh prince,
seconds away from handcuffed wrists
and inmate group showers.

I would have killed that girl.

Those rap songs you love to sing:

3 bitches, a new whip, and the green.
We prepared you for that,
but they're preparing you for this.

The defiant eye you had
when you realized none of your friends
had made the cut.

She feels she lost you
when you stopped holding open doors
and picked up that first cigarette.
The other gateway.

How do I communicate:

and yet you saved me
from the woman who raised you.
How do I return the favor?

You Might Be a Pickmeisha If...

If you still sign your brother's name at the bottom of the gifts you buy your mother. Every. Single. Holiday. Even though he's grown. And he lives with her. And you know not to bother asking for his share.

You might be a Pickmeisha if you've accepted a gift you knew was trash. Knew it meant he hadn't been listening to the uptenth hints you dropped. If you can accept how he can recall stats from sportsball in 1982 but still doesn't know a thing about you.

You might be a Pickmeisha if you sit next to your uncle (you know the one they don't let around the kids no more) at Thanksgiving. At Christmas. At the BBQ. Making sure his plate is warm. Knowing his ass wouldn't have a dollar for you if you needed it. They never do.

You might be a Pickmeisha if you don't blink when they ask if you have a good job, how much do you make, do you have roommates. And be shocked 3 months later when he's in your crib dropping just enough dick to dodge a contribution to the household. Nevermind he washes a dish. I don't wanna hear that he takes out the trash!

You might be a Pickmeisha if you've ever been left for a white woman. Sorry, any woman, and had the audacity to get mad at the other woman. Did she make vows? Did she promise you this lifetime and the next?

You might be a Pickmeisha if, when someone asks you about your relationship, you have a laundry list of what he did wrong, followed by, "but he's a good man." Sis, where?

— if you've been considering breaking up for 8 months now and just "can't." As if the only thing we can't take back is our time. Like he doesn't have to compete with you for yours. As if you wouldn't be better off alone.

— if you've been waiting on him to give you an orgasm and it's been a month! Imagine how long he would've stuck around if you didn't make him cum the first time. Much less the 18th. Fuck! The 52nd?

— if you've ever accepted a coffee date. I mean if your makeup costs more than his initial investment to meet with you, then you need to re-evaluate showing up. Any money he saves on taking you on a date just means he now has more money for someone else.

Matter of fact — you might be a Pickmeisha if you've gone half with a man. God forbid you pick up a tab. We don't make a quarter less than them to go half on anything!

— if you've ever answered the question, "what do you bring to the table?" Sis, you are the table!

Wake up. Start a meeting. Join a circle. Welcome to recovery.

Mlars

First impressions are everything, and I'm terrified of saying the wrong thing. Even after I've been braced, my neatly aligned teeth will fail to protect me from the reality of whatever comes out of my mouth. As they are largely designed to hold everything in. Only when my mouth is wide, risking exposure, will you ever see my molars. I always wonder if they're the reason my laughter brings pause. Unusually deep. Clenching. Trying to grind down milestones into easily digestible pieces. Their job is to prevent a choke.

Phlegm

I swallow the words I love you
like phlegm
struggling to be released
in a spasm of hacks,
assisted by bursts from my diaphragm.
My ribs are already spreading to prepare,
but no launch.
Instead I
strangle it back into my throat,
knowing one day
I will spit it out
at your feet.
It will end up
under your shoe,
like the rest of me.
Crushed.

It's the Disney Show

Scene: Curtains up. A Director and her two Brown Kids enter the Walmart.
They are all filed teeth and shiny foreheads, buttoned and tucked into
pressed jeans.

Mama said, "Shh... this is the Disney show."
She didn't mean the fireworks you could see from
our rooftop on the clearest of nights.
No roller coasters of screaming children,
no vibrant costumes,
and it sure as Hell didn't mean the happiest place on Earth.
She meant a different stage
in broad daylight.
The White People were watching.

Scene: Watch the Brown Kids dance in their stillness. See how their chests
do not even stir the air as they breathe.

I'm sure I used to throw tantrums.
I'm sure she used to pinch me,
scold me
not to touch anything.
I just don't remember it.

I know the result though.
My back snapping to attention,
my hands whipped to my thighs,
my mouth frozen into a smile.

Scene: Cue the orchestra as Blonde Girl in all white spins into chaos an aisle
over. Let the trumpets of her lungs build tempo. Feast on the tension between the two Brown Kids trailing behind their Director. Eerily in sync as they
back away, staring.

"Shh... the show must go on."
It still meant us in costume,
animated but not speaking,
hoping our gestures painted just the right picture.
It still meant screaming,
just internally.

Lord help us if we had a misstep
cause then it meant
waiting until we got home
to see some real fireworks.

Scene: The Director reaches the cashier counter. Soft drum roll here. Brown
Kid 2 reaches for candy as sirens grow louder in the distance. He is stopped
by the glare of Brown Kid 1. Sirens fade. Blue Eyed Cashier watches them
intensely as he scans groceries. Orchestra gradually softens. Brown Kids twirl
away to return to close proximity of their Director. Hanging on to her swinging
purse. Mute. Flutes and violins. They all make it safe to their car. It is black
and shining.

Either good or bad,
the curtains must surely come down,
followed by our shoulders.
Skin blending into the familiar blackness,
the lights will turn on the audience,
able to (finally) go
someplace else,
watch someone else,
and laughter can burst out of our mouths
live and in color.

My Story

I was never closeted.
"Girl stop playing around.
You're no lesbian."
This is from the mother who told me she'd love me
regardless of who I am
or what I choose to do.
This is after the seventh time I've told her.
This is with the illusion of hilarity
that I try to
force feed her
a dose of me.

My story is young.
Below four feet
and running with a girl my age
to the back room.
Giggly and cautious
underneath a yellowed comforter,
my little fingers
roam free.
We play,
kiss,
grab,
and squeeze
underneath, where we wouldn't be
heard or seen.

My story is boundless.
So I develop a crush on my boyfriend's brother's lover.
It moves past a desire
to map her curves
to uncharted areas.
Imagination running wild,
dates, discussions over books,
movies, eating at new places,
meeting new faces.
The idea of someone just
like her
by my side

is enough to make me eager.
If only just to please her.

My story is ravenous.
I'm devoted beyond mention,
lost and frustrated
around several thoughts rotating under a single idea.
Under her?
I want to give her the ocean,
watch the waves
put her in motion,
lifting her to heights
I've never been able to reach.
But as much as I fiend,
all I've ever been
is a host
to the dream.

My story is seen.
My favorite cousin,
and her curvy, milk skinned
girlfriend
pull me aside
to tell me what they already know,
what I already show
and give me all the answers
I need to grow.
A community spun from the forever shunned.

My story is a trigger warning.
Flashbacks constantly plague me.
Bits and pieces
of a picture so vague,
but insistent enough
to invade me
even now.
Swift enough
to evade me,
evidence of another time,
another space,
around ten.
At a friend's,

my panties a puddle on the floor.

My story is unfinished.
To this day,
my lips go unkissed,
missed
by those who I want
to enlist
on my team.
In all honesty, I wouldn't know
what to do with a woman
if I got the opportunity.
Could I even acknowledge,
let alone satisfy,
all of her needs?
Could I get over the fact
that it,
like mine,
bleeds?
May I never reach
a stage
so freed.

The Math in the Mantra
(I Think, Therefore I am)

People forget we did not ask for desegregation.
We asked for equality.
One plus one makes two,
but at the time it took three of us to equal you,
so how could me ever equal you?
It was a fundamental theorem
dressed in a language,
we have been force fed
and had to ask permission
in order to speak.
Punished by death if we want to read it,
jumping through hoops in order to reach it.
How dare you decide to not teach us
our history.
Descartes was never a slave,
but he made the mantra.
A reminder that
I do not have to ask you to think,
even while I do it to breathe.

Unrequited

I am no seed,
and you didn't care if I was
when you buried me anyway.
I am not kindling,
but you set me on fire anyway.
I am not stone,
but you skipped me anyway.

I will survive you,
and that is what is so terrifying,
that I bled myself at your frown
and the wounds didn't seal,
that I could so readily open my chest
and breathe for you,
that I still bear your charms,
solely weighted by their original intentions.

I'm going to carry you anyway,
long after you left my side,
even while you are heavy.

There isn't an end to this,
the door you closed on an open void.
May the fact that it is unlocked
tease you.
May it awaken you.
May the unexplored love
find you at night when you are alone
and force you to confront that it was
voluntary.

That you will have someone,
even unwanted,
who holds space for you
anyway.

Inherited Courage

Sometimes I am relieved to receive the option of a voicemail
– even after 8 hours, 36 minutes and 42 seconds
of buildup
to wish you a happy Father's Day
– instead of a text,
which would have been easier.
I can only imagine the reflected anxiety as you're only given four rings to answer
or to walk the twelve steps from the car to our door.
To come back in my life,
instead of turn around,
which would have been easier.
So I'll build up again.
Maybe it'll take me a couple more hours,
but it is in my genes,
apparently,
to hope past the discomfort,
which will become
easier.

In Her Defense
(Though She Never Asked For One)

I am the daughter of a side chick.
Also known as a breezy,
side piece, slide piece, or just
that other bitch.
But to me she is known as
Momma.
Allowed to give herself to a man
she did not own.
Not because she could make him moan,
but because she heard his groan
and erased his aches and pains.
Now I know I'm about to
piss some of y'all (first, second, and trophy wives) off
because she came first
and she'll definitely come after you.
You don't understand the attitude.
He doesn't choose her.
She chooses them.
But let's stand correct.
This is after she did the wife thing,
which most of y'all call the right thing
with a man who fathered both her only son and only daughter,
and he gave her all the love he thought he could offer.

Imma tell you what she taught me:
Creeping is hard work.
There's no such thing as a day off.
Instead there are weeks.
Then one day he calls and
you have to shut him down,
because he's on a rotation
and he missed his day last week.
Risking replacement.
You think this would displease him,
all she does is tease em.
She should probably leave them,
but she doesn't,
or she didn't.

Because 13 TVs in her house say
there is more than one way to apologize.

So while main wife
lives in strife,
denying her husband's second life,
I've never had just one father figure.
I am the daughter of a side piece.
I can play cards with the best of them,
throw the pigskin with the rest of them,
and don't have to carefully ask how to drive a stick shift
because she showed me the difference between
a wife and a dick lift.
And I know what I'm looking for.
Not money, sex, and at eleven the door.
Instead, I need a floor
(sorry), a foundation.
That's hard too.
Harder still to apply it
every morning.
Get dressed as if your
walking red carpets
and still worry about carpools and
European outlets for that vacation
you and your boo would have taken
if my mom wasn't already on it.

Sometimes dreams take priority
over societal demands.

She figured a way out of the box,
and just because she chose to follow her plans
doesn't mean I can't follow mine.
So get over it and get yours too.

Elegy to My Vagina

A rose in a garden
was supposed to bloom.
And it did, just late.
I clipped it,
and hid it away between bible pages
to save it from rotting away naturally,
to give it an excuse to feel important,
not grow
into something that doesn't matter.
Like mine did.
I lost it in a car,
doggy style.
To avoid the boy who became a man,
pumped into me
like his life depended on it.
Is this how a bitch feels?
Every time my dog
tries me,
he is caged.
I just ran to the swing set.
The only place even I grace
a bit of innocence.
But at that point, I couldn't get off the ground.
If it was the day before,
I could be heels off the floor,
face to the sky
and only almost there.
But you can't reach almost
with your legs closed.

PERMANENT

We only get 20 baby teeth to start with. That's 20 chances to figure out how to grow into your adult teeth. Everyone knows that these aren't permanent. Our starter teeth are meant to fall out to prepare ourselves for evolution. The whole set is meant as a trial run. What we choose to dig our teeth into, to attack face first, isn't stored in our oral history forever. Except that they are: our mistakes, the past. A set of well-documented teeth can be used to identify us, even after death. And we receive each one through biological, if not cultural, ceremony. A moment to celebrate each loss, knowing it brings growth. A rebirth. Which, try as they might, no one can prepare you for. What's worse is that no one can do it for you. Even if there were another Floridian Queer Black Womanist of the same pedigree, she wouldn't have a bite like mine. She'd have had to go through a life exactly as I have lived it and have received the same set of teeth with which to process it all. In permanence, only I get to do this twice. A second entire chance to not only prevent the mistakes from the first time around, but address them. The joke's on us though. The opportunity is still by design. And now being recorded in 32 teeth. A history of everything you've ever had to digest, documented in the hopes of identifying you, should you ever lose yourself. For real this time.

Incisors

I was always taught to chew with my mouth closed. That to open your mouth while something is in it reflects poor taste. We're not just talking about food when we say that. Everyone has to hold so much with their mouths. Quietly chewing over their problems, gossip, and secrets. And no one wants to see that. No one wants to witness the struggles you are still processing. No one wants to feel like they have to do something about it. You are on your own. By the time our adult teeth are setting in, most of us have mastered the art of hiding digestion. Just don't forget to smile while you do. It's rude.

Me at 21

I'm poly and confused.
It took me a while to get to that point,
to admit
that there's wiggle room here.
And here you are just trying to fit,
not satisfied if there's room for more than just you
or us.
But only in the way you see fit
for us.
You can't wrap your mind around how my heart can stretch
wider than your mom''s arms
when she said she loves you this much.
I'm trying to be patient and let you realize
you can't handle all of this on your own, boo.
I have a wishlist a mile long.
Why do you want me to place all my needs in you?
That sounds like stress.
That sounds like a mess.
That sounds like you're trying to become my ex.
I'm trying to live in a world without a next,
just additions
stretching to meet the true meaning of commitment.
You claim to be monogamous
but I'm the umpteenth girlfriend you've had.
Serial monogamy?
Contradictory.

Me at Done:
No, sir.
I'm bi. You're confused.
And sorry,
but you don't possess
world changing dick.
I've probably fucked more women than you.

Diana's Mother

I called my mother once,
let her know my motivation had fallen,
I was low
and didn't know which way was up,
I needed the reminder
that I am Wonder Woman.
She didn't laugh,
didn't miss a beat.
She asked me where my plane was.
And I,
not in the mood,
said I didn't care about a plane.
She said, "You can't just park a whole plane
just anywhere.
Who will pay for those parking tickets?
Remember where you parked the plane.
It will always take you home."
She said, "I love you."
I swore I heard it.

Past History

I'm still trying to get
past my history.
Trying to reverse a ripple effect,
a systematic triple threat.
A suffering from what no longer is.
A fight to be seen as different
than what was.
A family tree only three degrees of
separation
from the void.
"Who are you?"
they will ask today.
Not knowing my past story,
they'll just get the last story
that I have been told
three generations ago.
Then,
and now,
white space.
No family crest.
No rich heirloom chest.
No family beyond their manifests.
Do not ask where I am from.
It's history,
but won't stay in the past.

How to Heal a Previously Weaponized Body

Apologize to yourself.
Refuse complacency both indoors and out.
Refuse performative action.
Refuse to see your skin as additional weight.
Polish it when others use it against you.
Embrace the urge to remove yourself from those who do not enthusiastically
receive your presence.
Let the white people defend you for once.
Get some sleep.
Resume eating at scheduled times.
Prioritize pleasure.
Remind yourself who you are.
Pursue your self-care with rigor.
Organize when your heart calls for it.
March with others if your body allows it.
Listen and make space for the air
others may not be able to breathe today.
Breathe for them.
March for them.
Don't forget to reach back for yourself.
Make room.

Childish Ink

What if I told you I like
the feeling of being in your soiled sheets
a week after you left them?

If I told you that your children,
slain across my chest,
planted seeds for the greatest
self-pleasuring?

No one ever saw
me coming.

For the Audience of One

I'm sorry I had to win.
That I couldn't let you
believe you were right.
That I held you to a standard
higher than yourself.
That I wouldn't use your car
and would walk the walk to the laundromat.
But when you said,
"No one
could survive in LA without a car."
I chose to live as a reminder
of what your privilege was.
Chose to live in the space between us.
Forever performing for you,
demanding the recognition
that even our friendship
required me to work
twice as hard
to receive half as much.

A Whole Life of "No" Lives in My Mouth

There are two children, average height,
braces and college tuition to boot
set up behind my wisdom teeth.
I was supposed to have them removed,
the molars and the kids,
by a doctor,
but I didn't.
Just kept them in my mouth.
Swallowed them,
and breathed through another day.
Birthed new opportunities:
a career,
Roth IRA,
travel.
Stole my life back
from bills coincidentally
the equivalent of the doctor's Miata.
The one he'll have to find some other sucker to pay for,
a sucker who didn't use their knees for a second opinion.
The cavity can hold more than just prayer,
leaving a bad taste in my mouth
like I bit my tongue because they'd rather stop my period
than end this sentence.
One way or another.
But for now, I hold no by my teeth,
have sex in creative ways,
will merge prophylactics with my foreplay,
brush my teeth after I spit them out.
Brace myself for the wisdom.
I refuse
life's alternative diagnosis.

Hurricanes

My mother predicted the natural disaster well in advance. She gave my brother and I years of warning. Your father is coming, and much like you do, we began to protect our home. We sealed our gaps with hugs, made sure we had enough laughter stored away to pull out for later when things got scarce, shook the dust off our backup plans, and agreed on where to meet if we were separated and had to regroup. Practiced patience.

The only time I've waited for a man to come back in my life was for my father. A Florida girl, all I ever knew was hurricanes. I expected thunder. I expected it to be so loud the fear would distract from the rain on my cheeks. The tears, a flash flood at my feet. I was ready for it to be extreme at a distance but drop in severity once it made landfall.

When the doorbell rang, he delivered an earthquake to my door with such grace. The earth would shake beneath my feet and I'd loose sight of the surface. Everything I thought was stable just wasn't. Isn't your foundation just supposed to be there?

What the weatherwomen don't tell you is that the storm started with the separation. The bands of rain are every sad smile, every tear they wipe away, every time they hear, "Where's daddy?" Eventually they spread apart. You start to think it's just a spot of rain.

But I didn't have the ability to take cover, much less look for my brother who I assumed was right there. But my sibling was becoming a tornado. Whipping up too quick for my mother to sound an alarm. It's true that it sounds as loud as a train leaving the station. My father never had a chance to buy his ticket. My brother vanished as quickly as my father arrived. Flattening anything in his path, ending somewhere in his room. A closed door. He's never spoken to my father again.

An eye of a storm is a brief hour of reprieve. You imagine yourself through the worst of it. You remember you have more family than you can count on your fingers to power you through any outage. As my dad sat in the living room, swallowed up by all that had once given me comfort. He is the eye. A constant reprieve. Celebrated. Deceptive.

My mother goes unnoticed as a dormant volcano. We mistake hardened lava for soil. Assume safety in relics of bridges she burned for her freedom. She is erupting as he receives the spotlight for a damn return. No one compliments how her sulfur never rises, how she maintains her peace. She performs as weatherwoman because the aftershocks are rolling through my stomach. I'm heaving. What I hoped would be the exit of separation anxiety and daddy issues just looks like vomit. My mother holds my hair. She is my bathtub, my overturned mattress, my solid archway. She knows how to weather this, she's seen this before as her mother did before her.

With all storms, the weatherwoman is only ever half right. No one blames her for the aftermath. The damage is unpredictable that way. She will pan over her children as we put the pieces together, as we rebuild our home, even when all we ever talk about is the storm.

The weatherwoman knows that a hurricane is a bunch of thunderstorms that are just a bit too close together. She knows they'll eventually spread apart. She teaches me to spot the patterns. How the storms will leave and come back with yet another category, with yet another name, and they will pass. And there will always be the next weatherwoman to report that there's still silver linings. I will teach my daughter that the sun will shine again.

Canines

Around the time they were telling us it is impolite to bite people, I was told I smile too wide. A proper smile shouldn't show the canines. It looks uncivilized, wild. And a pretty girl like me should be able to hold her smile for the length of a picture. But if I smile too wide, then I'll spend much longer than the initial snapshot apologizing for the memory. For reminding people that behind my smile is the possibility of a bite. Heaven forbid I actually use my teeth on someone. It's not that biting people is altogether wrong. It's that it causes harm. Regardless of intention, using my canines can cause harm. Even as an adult, I am afraid that's what I'll be remembered for, the pain I caused for the split second I was out of character. Regardless of if I was trying to capture a picture. I will be held accountable for showing my canines. Still sharp. Still cornering. Still followed by apologies.

When He Doesn't Pick Up the Phone

I get limited issues
from this man who promised to pick up
where another had left off.
Be my father,
even backdated,
he volunteered.
Wanted me.
So I tried my best to be his favorite daughter,
as he has volumes of children,
of no fault of his own, of course.
Everyone except me knows he's human,
that this man isn't the difference between life or death.
Nevermind that I don't know life without him.

His breathing was my first playlist,
his snores, a nursery rhyme.
When my biological left
he came in right on time.
Carried my weight
easily
with a whole other wing for my brother.
A diorama of smile,
my bike crashed into his pickup truck stuck between the door
frames.
A quiet space for the tears he had the first time
I introduced him to my friends as my dad.
Even though we call him uncle,
even though there's no blood of his in my veins,
I'm still his brood,
his sequel
by choice.
I'd fight a thousand suns for him.

But one day I returned a call
and he didn't answer
for two weeks.
And just like that
I was at his knees,
an exhibit.

Trembling afraid
that something had happened to him
or worse,
if nothing had happened to him.
If he was just fine.
Breathing life into someone else,
living a lie somewhere else.
Preserved
without me.

Flipping through the archives.
I'm already withdrawing membership.
Denying the evidence,
demanding more sources,
detailing the footnotes of a past,
to heal a pain I know to be wary of
that hasn't even started yet.
I don't want to have to schedule a visit to see him,
check him out only to return him.
I don't want pain to fuzz our reception,
our connection destined to have gaps you can pass whole years through.
Trying not to touch anything,
and still not know what I could've done
to make him stay.
A told history,
repeating itself.

He eventually reached out
through mediums,
I found him in the lobby.
My nose behind
The Times.
A truck driver,
he knows how to deliver stale news
and I pick up the Highlights.
Excuses.
I consumed them wholeheartedly.
An aorta to the teeth,
blood dripping from my wounds.
I'm wailing.
Sounds like,

"Why do the fathers leave,
so that we have to work
to be rid of them?
Why do they come back,
still wanted?"
I can't tell the difference:
Is love a library
of stories
I need to finish?
Or a museum without a gift shop
and I'm always on tour?

April 19th 3:26am

Did you know it takes about three days of drowning in water to de-bloat and dilute ourselves for a man's tongue?
That there's just the right amount of mangos, pineapples and strawberries to have our juices sweet?
That there's a sweet spot for sex after shaving
(it's the night of and then exactly 3 days after that)
otherwise we're offering a soft pad to rub your cheeks against.
Which men should take as free exfoliation... but y'all stay playin'.
It's cool. I get it.
You don't know that we've bathed using all of our special soaps
and prepared for you with our fancy lotions
and put on our sexy playlist to get dressed for you.
That we do all of this.
For some three in one bath wash,
spray on deodorant,
and three songs worth of pumping?
Apparently.
So today I did not reach into my hidden bag
to line my wetness with cannabis infused oil,
the only thing that seems to mimic just how wet
I used to be for you.
It, at least, leaves me throbbing within the 15 minutes
of foreplay you used to offer me.
Today I decided not to manufacture the mood I used to be in promptly for you
because apparently men get tired as they near thirty.
Apparently sex is over after his orgasm.
Apparently he can't hold it because it's just too good.
So I've decided to advocate for my damn self.
I will buy another three minutes
by reintroducing condoms into our lovemaking.
Maybe yet another layer between us
will give you the right type of breakthrough.
I will tease another 5 minutes
by easing my back out of the arch I would sculpt for you.
Maybe then, the water will flow under the bridge you have to cross now.
I will retrieve another two minutes when I stop contorting from my shoulders
to moisten your sack from the back with my finger tips.
Maybe then your fingers will remember what it looks like to gently stroke
some slits,

arthritis be damned.
Because I refuse to leave another's ego as the only
thing that's being stroked properly around here.
Because trust me,
Imma get all of mine.
So today I did not reach into myself for my hidden tricks.
I did not open myself for you.
I didn't see the point.

[Insert Name Here]

Hey [insert name here],

I hope this message reaches you in good health. Unfortunately, we've exited the boundaries of simple conversation and this is now entering the realm of emotional labor. While I'm willing to educate you, which will directly benefit your status as an emotionally intelligent man and gain you opportunities previously closed to you among women, this will come at a premium. I can either send you an invoice, or upon me proving the accuracy of my initial statement, you can provide me with a gift. If not, feel free to argue with your mother about this. Be forewarned, if you feel the need to ask a man with a penis to back up my original claim before you believe me, there will be an additional charge for wasting my time and entertaining redundancy.

Peace and light,
Amon Elise

White Cishet Tinder Bio

Should read

Looking to date responsibly from a distance. Expect fancy Uber eats deliveries to your home and virtual romance. I empathize with your status in this country while recognizing the amount of effort it will take to undue the system that categorically benefits me. Challenge accepted. Yes fats. Yes femmes. Black lives matter.

Instead reads

Won't ask you to take off your skin
before entering the bedroom,
but will expect you to see
my privilege as the emperor's new clothes.
We will ride everything else
but the elephant in the room.
Mask optional.

Oh. And likes to travel. And here's the fish he caught. Height included because he guesses it matters.

Premolars

Funny how no one mentions that your teeth change your voice, how whatever sounds you make, must first echo off the geometry of your mouth. I don't remember there being anything wrong with my teeth exactly, just my mother and my dentist hovering over my open mouth discussing the benefits of getting braces now vs. doing so in the future. My future, which was at stake. I had an overbite in need of correction, which would lead people to question my smile. I was growing still, which was a problem for the braces. My dentistry had never been an issue before, but apparently there were way too many teeth to start the work. So with the looming eruption of my wisdom (teeth), all the work of orthodontic uniformity could be threatened, leaving me with a frontline of jagged teeth as nature intended. What better to eat you with, but not better for people to suspend disbelief in. Again, dangerous for my future. So they got rid of four of my premolars. It was unsettling. The idea of spare teeth that no one really talks about. Just a specific gathering of tissues that don't exist until your adult teeth start settling in. And that they could be removed to make way for further restructuring. Maybe if I kept the teeth, meant for crushing and grinding, it would have been easier to digest parts of womanhood no one wants to talk about. How others can just put their hands in you and change your voice from the root.

That was your trigger warning.

The First Man Who Loved You

When you meet him
the colors seem brighter,
there is a crispness to the air.
His detergent is cologne.
He brings you fruit.
He leaves you with hickies.
He carries your books to class.
You study each other.
You are young.
He brings you jewelry.
A snail trail is an understatement.
He keeps his promises.
The bear he brings you on Valentine's Day is taller than he is.
You pine for each other,
touch each other in stairwells.
Your first time is accompanied by music
and rose petals.
You go to different colleges,
but he still drives to take you on dates.
You talk marriage.
You've picked out kids names,
mapped out your lives,
and he's at every turn.

When he rapes you,
nothing hits the same.
You remember that statistic,
the one that tells you it's likely to repeat itself.
You can't sleep at night.
You realize his promises fall shorter than he is,
that his canines are yellowing,
that his laughter is too loud.
The next time you have sex, you don't feel it.
It takes you months to call a spade a spade.
You use words like
nonconsensual,
miscommunication,
accident.
Phrases like,

"Passion got outta hand,"
"He was desperate,"
"Sometimes it happens."
You take a left.
You can no longer recall the names of your future children
when he brings up marriage.
You remember that marital rape has only existed across all 50 states
as long as you've been alive.
You will need more than this lifetime to forgive him.

Summer Assault

Your fingerprints stained,
did you know?
Left imprints of wave-like indents
pressed against my skin.
Drowned me by the pull of the moon.
By the time it was new,
we had receded,
a sand of cells set adrift,
a ride in the past tense.
I haven't been the same since.

Coulda For Got

He ain't have no face.

Coulda been Gerald,
coulda been Steeve,
coulda been Reje,
but it was Kevin.

Knew it by the hand print
on my thigh's back.
Split themselves open

for questions,
for photographs,
for samples.

These men in blue
charged up to put em in orange,
made sure we all had it coming.

Got caught,
got fingered,
got processed.

Red Flags

Ain't I just a bunch of red flags?
And yet you're here
throwing a flag on the play
and coming despite the rules.

My red flags waved in front of you.
You charged anyway,
horns up,
stiff and ready
and fell for that bullshit.
Thinking you were aimed at me
and really I was aimed at you.

My red flags, you grabbed by the hips,
freeing me
by capturing it.
You told me there would be
no more games.

My red flags must be made of silk.
You go on and make your bed in them,
complain how you're trapped here.
Disbelief 'cause you didn't believe your ears.
But now is the time
to face your fears.
Next time
trust your eyes.

Cause ain't I just a bunch of red flags?
And yet you're here
throwing a flag on the play
and coming despite the rules.

He Came at Me

The first time he came at me I thought he was kidding.
The humping motion and grabbing at my clothes was a
tribute to 'drunk 18th anniversary was a month ago sex.'
He must be tripping,
and when I told him to slow down,
nary a change in pace was made.
My sensual stroke down his thigh
was ignored.
His hips just kept thrusting and his hands were grabbing
for my carefully selected underwear.

Bitch I used nair
for this.
I could've been your polyamorous guru,
introduced you to the new you.
Have you even heard of the word Nuru?

But it was consensual.
This isn't a rape story.
This is a second date story.
This is a we're watching movies at your crib,
I came in at midnight story.
I know what it is story.

He failed to recognize I was between a rock and a hard place
just because a mattress was at my back as he rammed into me.

Reluctantly put a condom on,
forced me to repeat myself.
Dryer than a Sahara dawn,
as this one apparently thought smegma was lube,
– dude.

I spent 16 minutes
rhythmically joining the ranks of women
who had proceeded me,
cursing them for allowing him to make it to 29 and be this awful at sex.
Which makes you single,
which is just another word for someone's ex,

or someone's swipe to the left
missing out in this chance to reconnect,

which is when you strip everything down and communicate
in a mother tongue or better yet with one,
but you withheld yours.
Only trumped by the fact that I held mine.

Afraid of what to say,
my mouth refusing to take shape,
and choosing to eat the word no
because I wouldn't be me if this was rape.

But I guess you weren't who I thought you were either.

When He Hurts Her

I hope you remember it on your wedding day.
I hope you hesitate the next time you invite him to your room.
I hope your breath catches the next time he asks you out
because he hit her,
and you said nothing.
And because you know,
no one would say anything to you.

When he hurts her,
I hope the next time you ask a girl to smile she flips you off.
I hope the next time you shack up at her house for the weekend she demands you contribute.
I hope the next time you bring chivalry up from wherever you've buried it,
she still questions your motives.
I hope you never again walk through life so confident
because you know even when she wasn't there
she heard your silence.

The next time he hurts her,
I hope I remember when he hurt me.
I hope I remember how when I called the police they decided not to take my statement because he didn't have any previous complaints.
I hope I remember I need to push to be the first
to say something.
I hope I remember to hold myself accountable
so that they will be held accountable,
all of them,
us,
finally.

Traveling Pants

When it happened for the second time,
I realized it had nothing to do with my jeans,
so when I had stopped eating
long enough to revisit them,
I was shocked at how easily my thighs
remembered the denim.
My stretch marks no witness to growth apparently.
The waistband hugged my hips in greeting,
but the trouble started at the fly.
The teeth refused to realign.
No matter how hard I tried to seal them again,
I didn't snap.
The mouth was open now,
gaping.
I thought it would be well received,
but the closure,
each tooth was jagged,
sharp,
threatening.
It would not hold me anymore.
It refused to hide me anymore.
It refused to be stored away on some shelf,
insisting to be the last defense to some other innocent
who hadn't yet joined the statistics,
who still thought old friends meant safety.
I dropped them off with good will.

Maybe I Should've Told Him

When your brother tells you the story,
you are not ever ready
because who is ever ready to connect those dots?
I mean, it's easy to see why someone would fall for my brother.
He is the first man I ever came to love, after all:
his laughter,
how tall he is,
the way he can set me at peace the second he walks into a room.

The story goes something like this:
His best friend takes a girl to prom.
There's a limo, a dance floor & spiked punch.
A hotel room is mentioned,
and my breath catches for the punchline.

Speaking of punchlines,
my rapist is 6'2."
His laugh is only louder than my own,
can make my hardships take their shoes off at the door.
When I tell you he turned everything I ever loved ugly,
know it to be true,
but back to the story.

The next lines are something like:
His best friend's prom is over now,
the woman is on his arm
using it as a crutch.
She's stumbling over her words, her plans,
her ideas for how the night will end.
Pause!

Maybe I should've prefaced that this story isn't far from my own.
Maybe I should've told him that I'd been raped.
Maybe I should've told my rapist
because this isn't the first time it's happened to me,
probably not to her either.
This is just the first time we,
I mean she,
I mean I

have chosen to speak.

But I'm getting ahead of myself.
Back to the story.

His best friend drags her into the elevator
which pulls her to the 14th floor,
and when she loses consciousness,
he fireman-lifts her without emergency
onto a bed
where he proceeds to...
tuck her in,
remove himself,
and shut the door behind him.

My brother has a smile creeping across his face.
Looks at me with such pride as he says,
"That's why he's my best friend.
He didn't even touch her,
just let her go.
He's such a good guy."
I dont have the breath to witness all the implications.
What does this say about the rest of his friends?
How the standards are so low to be a good guy
that...
that all of a sudden I can see my brother as a rapist.
Not a monster. Not a villain. Not an uncle.
But sibling!

We're both out of breath right now,
but mine is trauma-based, and he is laughing.
And we share that sound,
that echo,
our cheekbones,
a womb at some point,
that he has seemed to miss,
that both he and my rapist seem to miss,
that I'm not just someone's sister,
someone's daughter,
but a human whose value is not derived from her relationship to anyone else.

Because the girl in this story
is someone worth being too,
and she's not laughing either,
but I didn't say it
because then we'd argue,
and it hurts to realize the reason they go so hard
for the weinsteins, the Kobes, the Cosbys of the world
is because they recognize it in themselves.

But then again maybe I should have told him I'd been raped.
Maybe then he'd echo my distaste.
Maybe then he wouldn't be using our laugh
to mitigate a story not too far from my own.

But then I'd have to spare him the details I'm currently lost in,
like how my brother and rapist are the same height,
how they laugh from their bellies,
how they make me feel safe,
how they both worship the ground I walk on,
how they've met.
He and my brother
shared a room.
My brother and I?
Shared a womb
and how even my rapist has a little brother.

I pray his laughter
sounds as innocent
as he is.

M🦷lars

For the record. I have never cut my tongue on anything but a molar. Everyone is afraid of a canine, but
it's when your tongue is at rest or pushing food against
the teeth to aid in their battle for digestion that she is
caught in the crossfire. Your teeth aren't solely meant
to protect you. Sometimes they will leave you scarred.
Sometimes you are what is meant to be digested
and everything else has been getting in the way.

Do You Have Enough Space to Hold Me?

Here is my vulva.
Isn't she pretty?
I've never looked her in the eye,
but I'm willing to let you devour her whole.
May I trust you with her safe keeping?

Can I explore my throat with you?
Is it ok if only the two of us know how deep it goes now?
Can the only thing left to gag on
be the secret?
Can we seal it with a kiss?

I hope to echo it to the sheets, I guess.
They've been known to absorb more than a whisper.
Let us stain them in layers,
soak them in everything but silence
as long as it doesn't leave the room.

Our skins will know, too,
of DNA drying post percussion
of closeness.
Our largest organs
engorging, stretching
to meet each other,
a pinky promise?

But that's it.
This original dance,
without audience, is only on repeat
in muscle memory.
The persistent throbbing
an insistent mating call for a next time.
My ears in tune to your signature rhythm
sans hearsay.
Swear on your momma?

If I show you my open wound,
fresh from all who have betrayed our softness,

who found me just wet enough to slip through their fingers,
will it be enough to hold it between us two?

Autumn Chicken Bake

When it is The Girl Who Broke Your Heart's birthday,
I give you permission
to inhale her into your lungs.

Mix the poultry seasonings.
Take all the garlic she spit at you,
mix it with the vinegar she left in your mouth,
salt and pepper the chicken.
Try not to think about how seasoning
was always an issue.

Massage the mixture into the chicken thighs.
Let the guilt,
the sorrow,
the loss
marinate.
It will be a long night.

Chop up the damn sweet potato.
Use the shallots.
They taste better.
Tell everyone that you used onions.
They won't question the tears that way.

Split the brussel sprouts.
Try not to think about how clearly they divided.
Slice the apples
and add the diced maple bacon
to sweeten the blow.

Spray some pam so at least,
the residue will wipe away.
Try not to sink into the layers
and set to bake at 375 degrees.

When you're full of it,
of her,
evacuate your bowels
and shit.

Revolution

I am ready to start the revolution.
Are you coming ladies?
Repeat after me:
I will stop lying about my orgasm.
I will stop apologizing for my orgasm.
I will stop doing a disservice to all the women who will come after me.

The first time I knew I was a squirter, I was 19. I told him to hold on because it felt like I had to pee. Reje said, "Trust me and release," but I didn't because he was a nigga. Someone else's nigga at that. Maybe part of me knew to wait for someone who valued me as much as I do myself.

Dictionary.com lists an orgasm as a verb without an object. Ex: to have an orgasm. As if having them without an object is easy. Like I've never had to introduce my vibrator to my parents. He always has just the right vibe. Just my speed. Doesn't care about what other men I'm thinking about when I'm with him. In fact, he encourages it. It was perhaps my biggest epiphany.

Bing dictionary result reads: an orgasm is a climax of sexual excitement, characterized by feelings of pleasure centered in the genitals and (in men) experienced as an accompaniment to ejaculation.

They make sure to put the "in men" part in parenthesis as they want you to forget about me. Act like I don't exist. Like squirters are so rare we must be excluded by definition from receiving our highest pleasure. I should apologize to Reje as it would take another five years to find a man who cared about my orgasm. Curled his finger like he was Captain Hook after my childhood innocence. Took turns plundering and licking my openness. Knew the only way to make a lioness salivate is to feed it meat.

According to Merriam Webster, an orgasm is an intense or paroxysmal excitement especially: the rapid pleasurable release of neuromuscular tensions at the height of sexual arousal.

The only neuromuscular tensions men have ever brought me is stress. Trying to hide my shame. Told to keep it quiet. Held it down to not make a mess of myself on his sheets. Didn't wanna be a stain, didn't wanna be a bother. Held it down like my mother did when she left my father. Like the excuse I've made for every man who failed to satisfy me. Learning that disappointment arrives when he does. Early. So I learned to speak up.

Thefreedictionary.com states an orgasm is the highest point of sexual excitement, characterized by strong feelings of pleasure and marked normally by ejaculation of semen by the male and involuntary contractions in the female.

So it is no coincidence that to reach our highest point we must break through multiple contractions.
So fuck your can't.
Fuck your shouldn't.
Fuck your couldn't.
Fuck your won't.

My orgasms make yours look like a bitch. Because my holy water is only for the truly parched and strong swimmers. So I ask you ladies, for the last time.
Are you coming?
Because they're out here.
Thirsty.

Do Not Return to Your Hoe Phase

Stop. Turn around. Don't light the match. It's a yellow flag. Teensy. Minuscule. So what? It's not cause for panic. No need to lace up for the Mach 5 switch up. This is a category 1. It's not that deep. As they just reminded you. It's ok. You're still safe. They aren't playing games. This isn't like the last time, nor the time before that. This is different. We're months in. We're ready to commit. So what if they're not? So what if they have different requirements to go steady. So what if you haven't reached them? It's chill. We can just fall back. Casually. If you stop giving as much, they'll notice and it'll get worse. So push forward. Into whatever more they may ask of you. They don't need to know the trigger. Your soft spots. Your weaknesses. They are entitled to their own standards. It's fine. You'll be fine. Now is not the time to notice things that never bothered you. Now is not the time to self-sabotage. Now is not the time to flinch and scurry. Get it together. Breathe through it. Love anyway.
Love, anyway.

How to Tell Your Man the Sex Could be Better and Still Keep Him

1. Bring it up when the stakes are low. Well past the point where the sweat has dried in the hollow of your back. After he has felt he gave it his all, but when there is zero chance of sex happening. Remove the pressure. So the conversation is nothing more than a conversation. Ex. When making breakfast the morning after.

2. Say a prayer. May it never turn into a challenge. May the layers that shield his masculinity be strong. May he not prove himself less than worthy of your gifts in the first place. May he not hit you. Fuck that. He better not hit you. Wish that mother fucker would.

3. Breathe. And breathe again. Until your spine is as stiff as you need his erection to be after round four.

4. Use the voice you use when you order a sandwich the counter boy thinks you can't handle. A bit shy, but knowing it's what you want. Try not to worry about what he'll think when you prove him wrong and devour it. Act as if it is certain he will stay when all that is left is the discards and honey dripping down your chin.

5. Don't be afraid to use diagrams or to reenact comedian skits to explain what you want him to do with his fingers while he does that other thing you like. Hold it for dramatic effect.

6. In fact, riddle your requests with compliments about the things he does that you do like. In a two to one ratio. Three to one if what you're asking for is a two to one in the bedroom.

7. Set out the tantra books in strategic locations. By the toilet, on top of the remote control, blocking his PlayStation. If he doesn't get the idea, at least he'll eventually ask why his wallet was a bookmark in the Kama Sutra.

8. You practice on yourself. Get all the stuff out of the way you're not sure if you'll like. When you've hit somewhere close to gold, add it to your wishlist. Self exploration can lead to a steady hand when you guide him or when you ask him to watch.

9. Show him the effort you put in for him. Take up jogging and when he asks why, tell him you want more stamina for him in the throws of your horizontal tango. Invite him to your yoga class. Do your kegel exercises with a weighted jade egg in front of him. Do the most.

10. If he doesn't listen. Don't be afraid to try again. With a new man.

How to tell your new man that you love him:
You don't.

You swallow that shit.

And when the tears come, you use that as a chaser.

Old Feelings

I just wanna go back to the old feeling.
Remember before you messed up? Remember how that felt? Remember when you could make me happy? When you just showing up was enough? Before I laid out an intricate set of obstacles between us? Before I used to question the authenticity behind your actions? That time where I used to trust you without thought? Without pause? Before the trust was irreparable? When the damage was nonexistent? That time when I was the same person? At that place where I didn't have to wrestle with insecurity at the intersection of the moments we shared? Whatever we were up to when we loved like the inevitable wasn't coming? Before you fixed your face to lie about it in so many ways until I couldn't believe you? Prior to your attempts to resuscitate our relationship? Preceding the need for immediate recourse? Well before all the chances? Remember when I loved you and you took it for granted that I was yours? The sacrifice of it all? Dead that. You've been promoted to friend. With prejudice. Good luck in your probationary period.

Torn

Contrapuntal Poem: Please read column A as a poem, then column B as a separate poem, then read across the columns as if they were one whole poem. A contrapuntal is really three poems in one

I see you there

        brother mine,

black sheep,

        of my blood.

Mine,

        but not treated right.

Oh colored boy,

        abandoned to the streets at night.

Hair thick,

        wild heart

like mine.

        So you can't be home.

Yet somehow,

        I pray

your wool,

        It'll keep you warm.

Worth more,

        because we still love you.

RIP to All the Conversations

RIP to all the conversations that died once I told them my prices,
the awkward pause after I tell them I won't argue for free,
the brief inhalation when I announce I won't do the emotional labor they've thrust on me.
When they realize I'm really just fine with taking the dick to-go,
the silent calculations when they notice they really cannot afford me
and figure out I cost more,
that there are better people I'm holding out for,
that I only present myself to those who don't worry about the price tag,
who enthusiastically put down their phones in my presence,
who spoil me with focus,
support my vision,
curate spaces for me to thrive,
provide financial assistance before I have to ask,
foresee a future for me beyond the now,
don't question my needs,
realize every great party has a door fee,
and my time shouldn't be free.
Would be insulted if I even entertained a sliding scale,
who want to find out what it really means to fuck a price tag,
who can get this lesson on the clock.
The same ones who know that,
while you took the time to hesitate
evaluate me,
decide if I was even worth it,
the price just went up.

Wisdom

If you listen to your dentist, they will tell you that the mouth is often too crowded to create space for the third molar. They will remove your nature that urged a third molar in the first place. Both nature and your dentist wish to spare you pain, but you will experience it anyway from your dentist up front or from life on the back end. Your teeth were never meant to be straight, but jagged, unpredictable. There is no room for vanity, behind the molar, just wisdom. We spend decades waiting for their arrival, only to pull them out when they make too ugly of an appearance.

Orbit

When the man you buried your safety in
makes his first mistake,
the one where he compares you to the moon
forgetting you're a sun
and the only reason she shines is in reflection.
Because you're present
in the moment,
in front of him,
don't grab the hoe,
don't radiate single,
don't burn.
The past is dead.
You're here to generate life.
Thaw the cold shoulder,
even if it is your own.
You've got planets to run.

How to Orgasm in Silence

Fuck they.
It starts the way it always starts
by excusing yourself
to the room where you don't have to perform.
In fact, allow the thong you've only ever used to perform
for masculinity, for patriarchy to release you.
Go to the mirror you use to consult yourself
and open it.
Search for lubricant.
It isn't there.
Instead go to the makeup cabinet.
The special makeup you reserve for yourself.
Thank your past self for showing up for your current self
by placing the lubricant there,
where it's supposed to be
amongst the other instruments that keep you happy, keep you sane.
Start off by lubricating yourself
right where you are standing,
before you even get to the bed you've prepped
because make no mistake,
while they snore, you are still busy,
and your foreplay demands urgent immediacy.
Use it to massage friction away from your favorite vibrator,
the one your fingers can find in the dark
by physical memory.
Bring the lube with you because you have time.
You've made time for yourself today
out of habit,
circumstance,
mistake,
because others forgot,
because you didn't.
Bring it to the nightstand
next to your erotic novels
that are never enough.
Serve yourself on the blanket
which covers the sheet,
which covers the fitted sheet,
which covers the plastic tarp you've placed just in case

you're ever ready to release
to make room for yourself on the mattress you bought
to make sure your backbone was supported.
Prepare to birth an orgasm.
Start at a low setting,
allow for breaks.
Give yourself permission.
Release the fart,
you know the one they don't even know comes before you can release,
then turn it up a notch.
Allow yourself to revisit lower settings.
There is room for growth.
Find your path,
your secret spot.
Open yourself,
not for review, but for you.
Let their snores be your playlist.
They're sleeping on you anyways,
forever sleeping.
Who needs them?
Split open for yourself.
Use too much of the expensive.
Forgive, because you're worth not worrying about a price tag.
Start again
as many times as you need to.
Make room.
Try new positions.
Don't get down if it turns out the bar is set higher than you thought.
Show up for yourself.
Make the noises and let them cum.
Bring extra toys if you need it.
Listen to your body.
Receive your body.
When you do cum,
I challenge you not to hide the evidence.
Exist
again.
Repeat.

Even in this,
this pleasure

(your self-gift),
remember to show up for your future self
and charge your vibrator,
so the next time you have to reach for release
it is ready
because you are ready
and prepared.

After the Honeymoon

There is a moment after the honeymoon phase,
when the candles burn out,
the roses wilt,
and the scent of sex and trust
actively dissipates from the air.
You will remember that
you're a bird of prey
conveniently after they've left
the window open,
bored of you. And you will decide
not to take flight,
build the nest anyway.
They will observe. This. You.
Witness your anxious hop back and forth
between cold feet,
the swallowed embarrassment
in choosing to settle down anyway,
in choosing them.
They will then feed you your pride
as if you are still an early chick
surviving from their mouth alone.
They will close the windowpain,
for you both intentionally decided to enjoy
the consensual capture
of a mutual release.

A Generational Victory

I've cried my mother's tears,
but less often than she
cried my grandmother's.
A victory,
however silent.
These are the hard won silver linings
in a storm cloud of a day.

A CL⊕SING

Remember me for my mouth.
When I am long gone
and the words have stopped echoing,
the pages have faded,
and all that is left
is a history cradled in my teeth.
Take note of my final introduction.
Floss each identity with pride.
Man-made
woman
kept sharp by my stressors.
When the blackness decays,
and I can no longer hold lovers
with my tongue,
prepare my smile for a final viewing.
Do not hide my gaps,
the lessons I yellowed to the grave.
Open my jaws wide for the inspection.
Do not shame the natural deep crevices of my wisdom
by mistaking the fillings for cavities.
The life they fed me wasn't that sweet.
Have I ground enough down to expose a nerve?
Make them see.
I have nothing to hide.

Acknowledgements

Thank you.

Thank you to Worldstage Press for believing in me and encouraging me through my first published book. In fact, multiple thanks to any press, journal or literary magazine that has ever published me. Additionally, a huge thanks to all my English teachers, my editors, and most importantly my readers.

Thank you to the poet squad both in person and online that have cheered me on from open mic to open mic. May we continue to make spaces for our voices to be heard.

Thank you to all the relationships, both past and present that have brought me to where I am today. To be honest, there are a bunch of people who deserve gratitude for their *ain't shit behavior.* Old roommates, lovers who ended badly, family and even some ex-friends made it into the book. The book is not about you, but you'll make it about you anyway. So here is something for you to talk about. All of you. Figure out which one you are, start a support group, just leave me out of it.

Thank you to my ancestors who have given me the gift of continuing their story both in breath and with the pen.

And thank you Momma, because I know you'll come for me if I don't thank you specifically.

About the Author

Writer, yogi and sensualist: author Amon Elise envisions poetry the ultimate medium of expression, forcing her audience to ask questions, examine themselves and practice radical vulnerability. Originally from Florida, Amon worked as poetry editor for the Florida Review literary journal and the Cypress Dome literary magazine. Graduating with a degree in English and creative writing, she went on to serve as editor for the Peace Corps Indonesia newsletter. Her poetry has been published in Another Way Round literary journal and A Teenagers Guide to Feminism. She currently resides in Southern California and is making a name for herself in the robust Los Angeles poetry community. Outside of running seasonal erotic open mics and open mic pop ups, she has featured for Get Loud Movement, Nous Tous art gallery and Sad Bitch Poetry Collective. Additionally, she is the founder of Poetplug, a multi-continental open mic event board on Instagram. Catch her on any given night at an open mic speaking truth, but usually on the steps of Da Poetry Lounge hyping up her poet squad. May her words move you.
Find her on Instagram: @amonelise

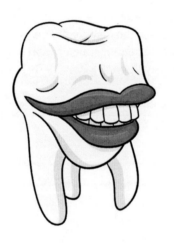